P9-CPZ-848

GREAT DISASTERS

# THE SINKING OF THE
# TITANIC

## JOHN DUDMAN

## Illustrated by Richard Scollins

The Bookwright Press
New York · 1988

# Great Disasters

**Titles in the series:**
**The Destruction of Pompeii**
**The Sinking of the Titanic**

**Titles to come:**
**The San Francisco Earthquake**
**The Space Shuttle Disaster**

First published in the
United States in 1988 by
The Bookwright Press
387 Park Avenue South
New York, NY 10016

Front cover: *Lifeboats full of survivors pull
clear as the* Titanic *sinks in the background.*

Words that are printed **bold** the first time they
appear in the text are explained in the glossary.

First published in 1987 by
Wayland (Publishers) Ltd
61 Western Road, Hove
East Sussex BN3 1JD, England

© Copyright 1987 Wayland (Publishers) Ltd

ISBN 0-531-18160-X
Library of Congress Catalog Card Number: 87-71744

Phototypeset by Direct Image, Hove, Sussex
Printed in Italy by G. Canale & C.S.p.A., Turin

# CONTENTS

# A SURVIVOR'S STORY

"There were men all around me — hundreds of them. The sea was dotted with them. I felt I simply had to get away from the ship. She was a beautiful sight then. Smoke and sparks were rushing out of her funnel . . . the ship was gradually turning on her nose — just like a duck does that goes down for a dive . . .

"The band was still playing. I guess all the band went down . . . I swam with all my might. I suppose I was 150 feet (46 m) away when the *Titanic,* on her nose, began to settle — slowly. When at last the waves washed over her rudder there wasn't the least bit of suction. It was very cold. I saw a boat near me and put all my strength into an effort to swim to it . . . I was all done when a hand reached out and pulled me on board . . ."

This was one survivor's account of the sinking of the world's biggest liner, the Royal Mail steamer *Titanic,* on April 14, 1912, after she rammed an iceberg on her **maiden voyage**.

Harold Bride, aged 22, from Nunhead, England, the *Titanic's* second radio operator, was among the 705 passengers and crew rescued after the liner plunged 10,000 ft (3,000 m) to the ocean floor with a death toll of 1,522.

The tragedy posed some questions. Why did this "practically unsinkable" ship sink? Why was the death toll so high? Why was she carrying too few lifeboats? These questions challenged the official **inquiries** held in the U.S. and Britain after the sinking and have intrigued the world ever since.

**Above** *Shocked survivors recover from their ordeal.*

**Right** *A news vendor cries the latest news of the tragedy that shocked the whole world.*

**Below** *A survivor is pulled aboard a lifeboat as the Titanic sinks in the background.*

HOW THE TITANIC WENT DOWN

# THE BIGGEST LINER EVER BUILT

It took a work force of nearly 50,000 men two years to build the *Titanic* at Harland & Wolff's shipyard in Belfast, Ireland. Everything about her was huge and comfortable. From the moment her **keel** was laid in 1909 the ship grew rapidly within a latticed scaffolding of plat-forms and cranes until she dwarfed the skyline around her, a proud silhouette with the sweeping lines of an ocean racing yacht. The *Titanic* was 900 ft (269 m) long, 92 ft (28 m) wide and her eight decks rose to the height of an eleven-story building. She weighed 46,328 tons.

**Above** *On the morning of the launch, the Titanic's hydraulic system is tested.*

**Left** *Workers leaving the Harland & Wolff shipyard. The outline of the Titanic can be seen in the background.*

6

Launched at Belfast on May 31, 1911, the *Titanic* reflected the mood of the **Victorian-Edwardian eras.** She combined security, luxury and confidence, and the sense of well-being that flowed from an unchanging society in which everyone knew his or her place. The accommodation for the rich, the middle class and the working class was clearly separated. She was the biggest liner ever built, and was certainly an example of the best in British workmanship. After all, about three million steel rivets had been slammed into that shining **hull**, with strong muscle and great care. Everyone agreed that she was the safest ship afloat.

A trade magazine, *The Shipbuilder*, described the *Titanic* as "practically unsinkable." This was based on her design for safety. Her three engines were fueled by 29 boilers built into 16 compartments, each one divided by protective **bulkheads**. In an emergency, watertight doors would fall like guillotine blades, sealing off each area. It was claimed that even with two compartments flooded there would be no danger to the liner.

**Below** *A cross section through the* **Titanic** *showing the layout of her* *decks.*

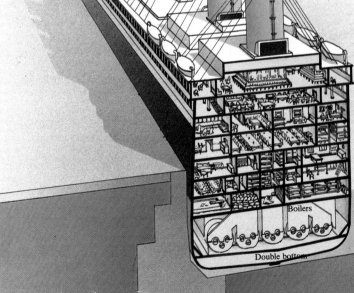

Lifeboats. The **Titanic** carried 16

A   First class lounge

B   First class dining saloon

C   Second class library and third class public rooms

D   Second class dining saloon

E   First, second and third class and stewards

F   Third class dining room and gymnasium

G   Swimming pool   Baggage

Boilers

Double bottom

# A floating palace

The statistics of the four-funneled *Titanic* were as impressive as her outline. Her enormous power plant produced 50,000 **hp** and ensured a top speed of 24 **knots**. And there was enough power left to operate a 50-line telephone exchange, the ship's radio, four elevators, a gym equipped with the latest in electrical aids to health, heating appliances for cabins, refrigeration units, cranes, pumps, winches, and a kitchen that was fitted with gadgets unknown in ordinary homes —

**Above** *Passengers relaxing in the comfortable surroundings of one of the elegant first-class saloons.*

machines that chopped, sliced, peeled and whisked.

But it was the *Titanic's* breathtaking passenger accommodation that made her renowned as a floating palace. It was planned by her owner, J. Bruce Ismay, chairman of White Star, an international shipping line. He wanted to combine elegance with spaciousness and speed.

The *Titanic* carried grand staterooms, luxurious suites and comfortable cabins for 2,433 passengers: 735 in first class, 674 in second class and 1,024 in third class.

On the first- and second-class decks there were tapestried dining rooms, where the menus equaled those of the best London hotels, quiet lounges and smoking rooms. Every night in the oak-paneled grand saloon, where plants grew and hidden lights shone through windows of gray glass, an orchestra played the latest ragtime tunes. The decorations in the libraries echoed the furnishings of ages long ago.

The first-class passengers strolled on their own private promenade decks or they lazed on **verandas** beneath the shadows of the four funnels towering 62 ft (19 m) above them. Higher still was the ship's antenna slung between two slender masts, one of them carrying the **crow's nest.**

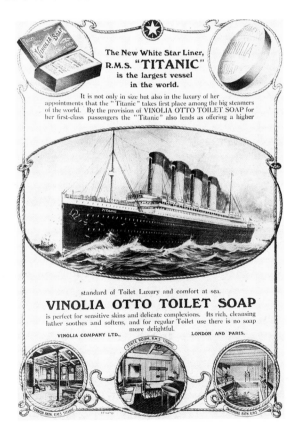

Above *J. Bruce Ismay, Chairman and Managing Director of the White Star shipping line.*

Above *An advertisement for Vinolia soap in 1912, praises the luxury of the White Star liner.*

## Comfort for all

Some of the first-class suites were warmed by coal-burning **Adam fireplaces,** with four-poster beds gracing the polished woodwork of the bedrooms. A grand oak and wrought-iron staircase 60 ft (18 m) high, with a central **balustrade**, linked the first-class decks. For first-class passengers, too, there was the first swimming pool ever installed on a liner and **Turkish baths** with gilded cooling rooms.

Other special facilities included a squash court, a darkroom for photographers wishing to develop their own films and, for everyone, barber shops with automated shampoos. A hospital equipped with an operating room was ready for any medical emergency.

Even on the lower decks the third-class cabins — known as "steerage" — offered exceptionally comfortable accommodation for the time, with four bunks and a washbasin to a cabin. Food was in more plentiful supply than many

**Below *Passengers enjoying the swimming pool and Turkish baths, two of the many facilities on the* Titanic.**

passengers had ever known. Parts of the third-class decks could be converted to **freight** compartments, a tradition from the days when traveling in "steerage" meant traveling with the baggage. Emigrants from Europe to America were carried "steerage" on the way out, and cattle occupied the same space on the return journey.

There was a big business motive behind the creation of the *Titanic* as a gigantic pleasure boat. For some years, European and American shipping lines had been competing fiercely for the transatlantic ferry traffic as increasing numbers of tourists — including many Americans — wanted to spend new-found fortunes traveling the world. They expected the best and demanded luxury with speed.

So White Star engaged Harland and Wolff, the most expensive but most reliable shipbuilder in Europe, to build their latest superliner. They were already building a sister ship, the *Olympic,* which made its maiden voyage on the day the *Titanic* was launched. The latest ships employed new technology: steel frames and powerful boilers were replacing the old wooden-hulled sailing vessels.

The *Titanic,* which weighed over 1,000 tons more than the *Olympic,* arrived in Southampton harbor in England on April 3, 1912, with high hopes of capturing the biggest share of the transatlantic shipping market.

**Above** *A little boy spinning a top in the children's playground area, on the saloon deck of the liner.*

**Above The** Titanic *is launched, stern first, into the waters of Belfast harbor on May 31, 1911.*

# THE MAIDEN VOYAGE

The *Titanic* sailed from Southampton on April 10, 1912, to the cheers of thousands of well-wishers on the shore and the shouts of others aboard a steamer alongside the jetty. A fierce **wash** caused by the *Titanic*'s suction snapped the mooring lines of the steamer *New York*. Spectators ducked as the steel **hawsers** whipped into the air. The *New York* drifted into the path of the *Titanic* and for a frightening moment a collision seemed inevitable.

On the **bridge** of the *Titanic*, Captain E.J. Smith increased power on the **port** engine and the wash sent the *New York* back toward the pier. The *Titanic*'s passengers, lining her rails, watched the incident with renewed confidence in their captain. No doubt he remembered that only six

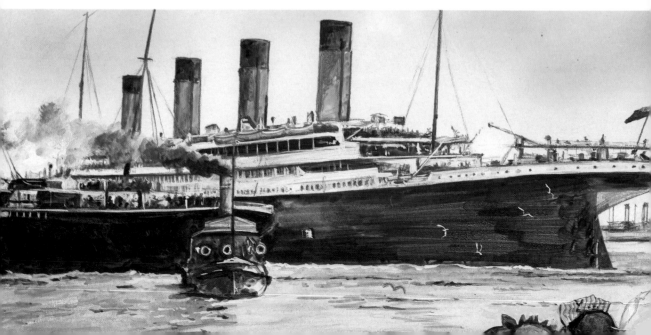

*Above The* Titanic, *photographed as she left Queenstown, Ireland, heading for the North Atlantic.*

*Left Captain Edward J. Smith, the highly respected but ill-fated commander of the* Titanic.

*Below At Southampton, a crowd waves farewell as the* Titanic *sets off on her maiden voyage.*

months before he was commander of the *Olympic* when she collided with a cruiser HMS *Hawke* in Southampton harbor which badly gashed the *Olympic's* hull.

The *Titanic* made two passenger and mail stops — at Cherbourg, France, and Queenstown, Ireland — before setting off across the North Atlantic. She carried 337 first-class passengers, 271 in second class and 712 in third class. The crew totaled 907. In her holds there were 3,435 mailbags, 6,000 tons of coal, 900 tons of baggage and enough food for several months.

As she headed into good weather, life on board settled down to the usual fashion of a luxury liner, with rich industrialists relaxing in sumptuous surroundings, and the lower deck passengers excited by their unexpected comfort and looking forward to the voyage. The *Titanic* was a happy ship.

## The rich and the famous

On board, millionaires abounded. The richest man aboard was Colonel J. J. Astor, owner of a string of plush New York hotels. He was worth many millions. Also on board was Benjamin Guggenheim, who made his millions manufacturing mining machinery, and there was Isidor Straus, owner of New York's famous store, Macy's.

On the evening of Sunday April 14, Captain Smith dined with a group of passengers and then went to his bridge. It was just before 9 p.m. The *Titanic* sped through a calm sea at 21 knots beneath a sky glittering with starlight. In the radio room, the chief operator, Jack Phillips, was receiving the latest of several warning signals from other ships that the liner was heading into ice fields. An unusually warm winter had caused many icebergs to break away from the Greenland coast and move into the shipping lanes off the Grand Banks, southeast of Newfoundland.

## Iceberg warnings

On the previous Friday — two days out of Southampton — the *Titanic* received an iceberg warning from a

*First-class passengers, Colonel Astor (large picture), Lady Rothes, Lady Duff Gordon, Major Butt, Benjamin Guggenheim (in order clockwise).*

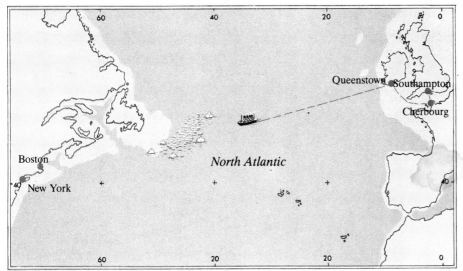

**Left** *This map shows the route taken by the* Titanic *on her fateful maiden voyage.*

**Above left** *Radio operator Jack Phillips.*

**Above right** *Karl Behr, famous lawn tennis player and ex-captain of Yale University.*

**Above** *Mr. Isidor Straus.*

French liner *Touraine*. Captain Smith telegraphed his thanks. At 11:20 a.m. that Sunday, Phillips intercepted a message from a German ship and informed Captain Smith. He ordered Phillips to relay it to the U.S. Hydrographic Office in Washington, D.C. It said: "The German steamer *Amerika* reported by radio-telegraph passing two large icebergs in **latitude** 41°27', **longitude** 50°8' — *Titanic*." As midnight approached, more **Morse** signals were beeping more alarms into Phillips' headphones. He notified his captain. But the *Titanic* did not slacken her speed . . .

In the crow's nest high up in the forward mast was the lookout, Frederick Fleet, aged 25. He shivered as the temperature slowly dropped to freezing. The binoculars that were usually stored in the crow's nest had been taken down to the bridge.

# COLLISION

At 11:39 p.m., Fleet saw a faint, dark shadow approaching. He rang his alarm bell three times, snatched up his telephone and called: "Iceberg right ahead!" "Thank you" came the reply.

Grasping his telephone, Fleet watched the shadow looming larger and larger. The *Titanic's* **bow** began to move to port as the top of the iceberg towered high above the liner and then scraped its **starboard** side, showering the decks with ice. In ten seconds it was all over. Six watertight compartments were pierced. The sea poured in. The time was 11:40 p.m.

Few passengers realized immediately the peril they faced. They had complete confidence in the *Titanic*. But Captain Smith knew that with so many compartments opened up there was no hope. He ran to the radio station and ordered Phillips to send the international telegraph call for help.

The Morse buzzer tapped out the distress signal "CQD." Harold Bride nudged Phillips. "Send SOS," he said. "It's the new call and it may be your last chance to send it." It was.

The Cunard liner *Carpathia* was about 48 miles (80 km) away when she

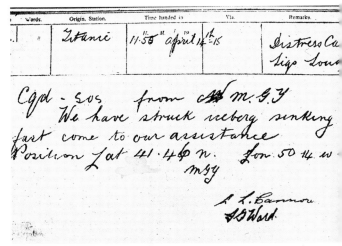

| Words. | Origin. Station. | Time handed in | Via. | Remarks. |
|---|---|---|---|---|
| " | *Titanic* | 11.55 M. 1 april 14 15 | | Distress Ca Sigs Loud |

Cgd - SOS from M.G.Y
We have struck iceberg sinking
fast come to our assistance
Position Lat 41.46 n. Lon 50 14 w
mgy

L. L. Cannon
H.B. Ward.

**Above** *The message received by the* **Birma** *five minutes after the collision.*

**Left** *Jack Phillips taps out the SOS message that the* **Titanic** *is sinking.*

**Below** *Frederick Fleet tries to warn the bridge of imminent danger as the iceberg looms ahead.*

picked up the world's first SOS message. She immediately changed course and raced to the *Titanic's* position: 41°46′ North, 50°14′ West.

The *Titanic's* corridors were teeming with passengers and crew as the news of the collision spread through the ship. Lifeboats were made ready with passengers lined up according to the law of the sea: women and children first. There was no panic. Husbands kissed their wives and children farewell and then stayed behind on deck.

## Into the lifeboats

In the tilting first-class lounge, men played cards, drank their last drinks, and then joined the other passengers, wearing lifebelts over their evening dress as they paraded with slow dignity down the grand stairway and out onto the listing decks. The orchestra was playing ragtime.

Above the liner, distress rockets swished skyward, bursting with white stars. Somewhere over the horizon they were seen by a 6,000-ton ship, the

**Above** *First-class passengers wearir lifejackets over their finery file calmly down the grand staircase.*

*Californian.* But her skipper, Captain Stanley Lord, failed to go to the rescue.

As the *Titanic*'s lifeboats were lowered 69 ft (21 m) to the sea below, the passengers were calm. Benjamin Guggenheim appeared on deck resplendent in his finest evening clothes and told a steward: "Tell my wife, Johnson, if it should happen that my secretary and I both go down and you are saved, tell her how I played the game out straight to the end. No woman shall be left aboard this ship because Ben Guggenheim was a coward." Colonel Astor helped his pregnant wife into a lifeboat. Then he stood back calmly to await his fate. So did Major Archibald Butt, friend and aide of the U.S. President, W. Taft, and Isidor Straus and his wife. Mrs. Straus was ordered into a lifeboat, but she declared: "I will not leave my husband. We have been together all these years and I'll not leave him now." She waved farewell and then she and her husband settled down in deck chairs.

Aboard one lifeboat, however, was J. Bruce Ismay whose conduct was later criticized at the official inquiries. He **testified** that no women were left on the deck when he entered the lifeboat.

**Above** *Women and children are helped into a lifeboat.*

**Left** *Husbands and wives say goodbye on the deck of the sinking ship.*

"The starlight night was beautiful"

Stern
2nd class
Section of ship

Boat Deck
clear of boats

Titanic looked
enormous

Every porthole
& saloon was
blazing with light

bows & bridge
completely under water

"We had sixty
or seventy
on board"

"Sea calm as a pond
There was just a gentle heave"

J. McFarlane

*Left A painting based on an eye-witness account of the* Titanic's *final moments. The lifeboats are full, with hundreds of people still left on board the liner.*

# The end of the *Titanic*

Charles Lightoller, the *Titanic*'s second officer, who marshaled passengers into many lifeboats, was on top of the wheelhouse when the liner pitched forward. He dived into the icy water only to be sucked toward an airshaft. As he clawed at a wire grating, a blast of hot air threw him free. In the darkness, he felt more suction and swam frantically to escape. Suddenly he broke surface beside a lifeboat. He was pulled in and, looking up, he saw the **stern** of the *Titanic* rearing high into the sky. Hundreds of people were packed on the stern deck where two priests were crying: "Prepare to meet God!" The band was still there. The melody of a hymn floated down to the lifeboats and the flagging swimmers struggling in the freezing water.

From the towering stern, passengers joined hands in groups and pairs and leaped from the almost perpendicular superstructure. Explosions shook the *Titanic* as the boilers and engines were wrenched from their foundations. Her lights cast a strange glow in the water as they dipped beneath the surface. Then she began her slow descent to the bottom of the sea leaving a mushroom cloud of smoke and steam over her grave. It was 2:20 a.m.

The *Carpathia,* under the command

of Captain Arthur Henry Rostron, reached the scene as a pink dawn tinted 20 miles (32 km) of icebergs and floes. The lifeboat survivors and those who died beside them that night were taken aboard the *Cunarder,* which set sail for New York. Hundreds of other bodies of people frozen to death were picked up by passing ships in the weeks that followed the disaster.

**Left** *A lifeboat full of survivors is hauled aboard the* **Carpathia.**

**Below** *The* **Carpathia** *was the first ship on the scene of the tragedy.*

 # THE INQUIRIES

The *Titanic* tragedy shocked Britain and the United States out of their smug complacency. People everywhere felt that the Atlantic Ocean had produced a fearful omen that night. It seemed the world would never be quite the same.

Official inquiries were held on both sides of the Atlantic into the cause of the catastrophe. Some questions could be answered, some could not. Certainly it was accepted that the *Titanic* was carrying too few lifeboats, although the

**Left** *Stunned relatives gather outside the White Star offices in Southampton desperate for news of their loved ones.*

owners complied with **Board of Trade** regulations, which decreed that any vessel more than 15,000 tons in size should carry no less than sixteen life-boats. There were twenty lifeboats on board the *Titanic* but they could take only 1,178 people — more than 1,000 short of the number of passengers on that maiden voyage.

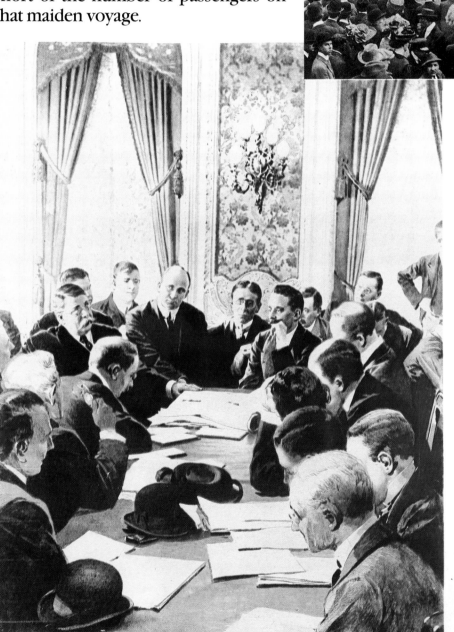

**Above *Crowds outside the* New York American *newspaper office wait for the news.***

**Left *J. Bruce Ismay (top right of table) giving evidence at the U.S. inquiry.***

23

The inquiries were unable to explain why Captain Smith, who died with his ship, failed to slow down after receiving those iceberg warnings. He was not attempting a record-breaking run, since the liner could not match the speed of smaller ships. If his seamanship was questionable, his behavior as a captain after the collision was perfect. The London court refused to condemn him since he could not defend himself.

The evidence also left unsolved the mysterious role of Captain Lord of the *Californian,* who claimed that there was another ship between him and the *Titanic*. But the inquiries found that there was no discrimination among passengers on board, although why as

**Above *Captain Stanley Lord of the* Californian.**

**Left *A crewman gives evidence at the London hearing.***

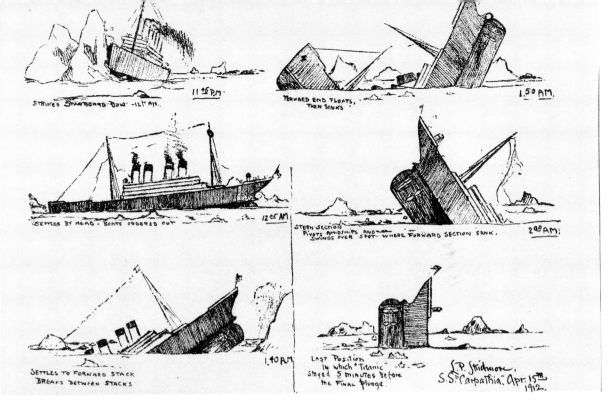

STRIKES STARBOARD BOW –12.1ST A.M. | 11.45 P.M.

FORWARD END FLOATS, THEN SINKS | 1.50 A.M.

SETTLES BY HEAD – BOATS ORDERED OUT | 12.05 A.M.

STERN SECTION PIVOTS AMIDSHIPS AND SWINGS OVER SPOT WHERE FORWARD SECTION SANK. | 2.00 A.M.

SETTLES TO FORWARD STACK BREAKS BETWEEN STACKS | 1.40 A.M.

LAST POSITION IN WHICH "TITANIC" STAYED 5 MINUTES BEFORE THE FINAL PLUNGE.

L.P. Skidmore, S.S. "Carpathia" Apr. 15th 1912.

**Left** *Alexander Carlisle, the Titanic's designer, arriving at the court of inquiry in London.*

**Above** *Drawings by a survivor of the Titanic's end. They were presented in evidence at the hearing.*

many as 100 women died when some lifeboats were not full could not be answered.

The courts of inquiry led to improvements in safety at sea, ensuring that enough lifeboats would be provided for all passengers, that all ships would carry radios, and that the U.S. Coast Guard would establish regular ice patrols, funded by thirteen countries.

25

# DISCOVERING THE WRECK

More than seven decades passed before the wreck of the *Titanic* was discovered embedded 55 feet (15 m) in the Atlantic seabed. In the autumn of 1985, an American-French expedition succeeded in pinpointing the liner's last resting place.

Dr. Robert Ballard, a scientist with the U.S. Ocean Engineering Department, led the expedition. He had been inspired and helped in his quest by the Titanic Historical Society of Springfield, Massachusetts. The French group was interested in testing new **sonar equipment.**

The wreck was found in September, 1985, about 350 miles (500 km) southeast of Newfoundland. Nine months later Dr. Ballard and two colleagues were positioned over the spot in *Atlantis II,* the mother ship of their small deep-sea submarine. It took more than two hours to descend to the seabed about 3 miles (5 km) below.

As the submarine neared the ocean floor, the three men saw their searchlights pierce the darkness and pick out a wall of black steel. They skirted the rust-encrusted bow and explored the foredeck, glimpsing unbroken portholes, and discovered that just behind the third funnel, the *Titanic* had split apart.

**Above *Divers from the U.S. Ocean Engineering Department stand on top of their deep-sea submarine.***

One-third of the liner was missing. The stern was about 165 feet (50 m) away at the end of a trail of debris.

**Above** *Jason Jr.,
a robot
equipped with
cameras, swims
off along the
side of the
Titanic.*

**Right** *The
remains of a
chandelier,
photographed
by Jason Jr.*

## Sunken treasure

On the third trip, Dr. Ballard took a self-propelled robot equipped with cameras. The robot, attached to a 250-foot (75-m) line, set off into the murky interior of the *Titanic*. Its cameras focused on the grand stairway, where the beautiful woodwork had been eaten away. But in the lounges, exquisite glass and crystal chandeliers were still hanging perfectly intact. Stalactites of rust had formed on the ceilings. The wood of the ship's wheel had vanished but the gleaming brass fittings were almost as good as new.

The robot continued its investigation, past anchor chains into the gymnasium. It inspected the officers' quarters and moved up the forward mast to the crow's nest with its trailing telephone line. All around was the chaotic bric-a-brac of disaster: heaps of coal, brass pans, chamber pots, bottles of wine, a shoe, a safe.

But there was no sign of a huge gash on the starboard side, a discovery that shattered the myth that the iceberg had cut the hull wide open. The steel plates were buckled and the steel rivets missing, suggesting that they had shot out like bullets when the collision occurred.

Dr. Ballard surfaced with thousands of camera shots to examine. He ruled out any possibility of salvaging the *Titanic*, having decided that any movement of the remaining wreck would mean its loss entirely, because the ship would disintegrate under the tremendous pressure of the sea.

**Left** *This deep-sea photograph shows two bollards, used to secure mooring lines, and the ship's rail still remarkably intact after more than 75 years under the sea.*

Left *Seven-year-old Eva Hart, a* **Titanic** *survivor, with her parents in 1912.*

**Below** *Photographed during an interview in 1985, Miss Hart, aged 80, said she was against any attempt to raise the wreck from its final resting place.*

## Always remembered

So the *Titanic* will remain in her ocean grave. But she will never be forgotten. The **flotsam and jetsam** brought ashore rests in museums in the U.S. There are official documents in archives, and memorials in Southampton, England and in Halifax, Canada, where so many bodies were unloaded from ships. In 1987 a French salvage operation began to retrieve items from the wreck of the *Titanic*.

On April 14 every year an American Coast Guard boat has always dropped a wreath on the Atlantic in memory of the *Titanic*. Now the crew will be able to cast it over the exact spot.

# GLOSSARY

**Adam fireplace**   Decorative fireplace designed by Robert and James Adam of England in the eighteenth century.

**Balustrade**   Row of posts joined by a stair rail.

**Bow**   Front part of a ship.

**Board of Trade**   Now the Department of Trade and Industry. The British government department responsible for policy affecting trade, public bodies and consumer protection.

**Bridge**   The place on board a ship from which it is piloted and navigated.

**Bulkhead**   A wall-like partition.

**Crow's nest**   A lookout post on a ship's mast.

**Edwardian era**   The years from 1901 to 1910.

**Flotsam and jetsam**   Debris from shipwrecks found floating on the water.

**Freight**   Heavy goods.

**Hawser**   Heavy ship's rope.

**HP**   Horsepower; the power a horse can exert.

**Hull**   The main body of a ship.

**Inquiries**   Investigations held to discover the cause of an incident.

**Keel**   The main part of a ship's framework.

**Knot**   A nautical mile, or unit of speed equal to 1.15 mph (1.852 kph).

**Latitude**   A place measured in degrees north and south of the equator. Shown on maps as horizontal lines.

**Longitude**   A place measured in degrees east and west of Greenwich, England. Shown on maps as vertical lines.

**Maiden voyage**   A ship's first journey.

**Morse**   A code used in signaling in which each letter is represented by a combination of dots and dashes. Invented by Samuel F. B. Morse (1791-1872).

**Port**   The left-hand side of a ship.

**Sonar equipment**   Equipment that uses sound waves to find an object.

**Starboard**   The right-hand side of a ship.

**Steerage**   The cheapest cabins on a passenger ship, usually on the lowest deck.

**Stern**   Back part of a ship.
**Testify**   Gave evidence under oath.
**Turkish bath**   A steam bath.
**Veranda**   A roofed gallery or porch.
**Victorian era**   The years from 1837 to 1901.
**Wash**   Waves or wake made by a ship.

# FURTHER INFORMATION

There is a great deal of information on the *Titanic* in books and articles. You might be interested in the following books:
*Night to Remember* by Walter Lord. Bantam Books.
*Ships and Other Seacraft* by Brian Williams. Franklin Watts, 1984.
*The Story of the Titanic as Told by its Survivors* Jack Winocour, ed. Dover, 1960.
*Titanic* by Richard A. Boning. Barnell Loft, Ltd., 1974.
*Titanic* by Frank Sloan. Franklin Watts, 1987.
*The Titanic Revisited* by Leo Cohen. L. Cohen, 1984.

Your local library may have copies of newspapers reporting the disaster at the time. The Titanic Historical Society in Massachussetts keeps the most up-to-date records and information on the disaster and the recent rediscovery of the wreck.

# INDEX

# ACKNOWLEDGMENTS

The illustrations on pages 7 and 15 are by Malcolm S. Walker.

The publishers would like to thank the following for providing the photographs in this book: Mary Evans Picture Library COVER, 5, 19(t), 20; Illustrated London News 5, 9, 12, 17, 19(b), 22, 23(b), 24, 25(b); Harland & Wolff 6, 11(b); Peter Newark's Western Americana 21, 23(t); Popperfoto 11(t), 13, 14, 17(l), 27(b); Topham Photo Library 14, 15, 25(t), 29; Woods Hole Oceanographic Institution 26, 27(t), 28.